Anthology I

Poetry

by

PAT JOURDAN
MAUREEN GALLAGHER
TRISH CASEY
SUSAN MILLAR DUMARS
BETSY CARREYETTE
CAOILINN HUGHES

Edited by Deborah Evers & Kevin Higgins

ᛉ
Ainnir | New Writings

Published in 2004 by

Ainnir Publishing
Kinvara
Co. Galway
Ireland
ainnir@eircom.net
www.ainnir.com

Copyright © 2004

ISBN 1 901109 05 4 Paperback

Cover Image: *Joy* by Corrina Askin
Cover Design and Set by: Helen Larrissey
Printed by: i-Supply, Galway

Acknowledgements

Rita Ann Higgins
Pat Boran
Todd Swift
Josephine Vahey, Galway City Library
Scribbles Cafe and Wine Bar
Maura Kennedy and Tomás Hardiman of the Galway Arts Centre
Helen Larrissey, Postscript, Kinvara
Louis Donnellan, i-Supply, Galway

Publisher's Note

Is le héirí na maidhne tháinig ainnir fá mo dhéin le póig;
(Úirchill an Chreagáin le Airt Mac Cumhaidh 1715-1773)

Ainnir Publishing is a cooperative. The income generated from the sales of these books, after costs, goes towards producing the next publications. The aim is to give new writers the opportunity to have their first work published in order to give them encouragement and a literal stepping stone towards having more work published by other publishing houses. It should be noted that this opportunity is open to writers who have already been published in another medium, but wish to publish a first work in a new medium. The writers must be seen to have made efforts to develop their writing skills or have had one or more pieces published. The work should be supplied in hard copy and on disc. The intention is that the writers help themselves by helping the cooperative.

This year we have just launched our website at www.ainnir.com. *Anthology I* is being launched at the *19th Cúirt International Festival of Literature 2004* and later in the year we will launch the *Cathal Browne New Writer's Award.*

It is hoped that we will be able to afford many new writers the opportunity to have their work published. To date we have published four volumes;
The Water is Wide, a profile of 13 Irish artists, *THE ADVENTURES OF PUCK,* short stories by Cathal Browne, *AFTER LORCA,* poetry by Molly Gowen and *No Vague Utopia*, poetry by Emily Cullen. It is difficult to continue to publish without production support. We are seeking support for our publications and hope to receive some funding for future development of new writings.

In the light of this, your support, through purchasing these works, is appreciated. I hope you enjoy this book.

Deborah Evers
Ainnir Publishing
April 2004

Preface

The six very different voices in this anthology spark off each other, creating a dramatic fusion that acts as the structure of the volume. This amalgamation enables the poets to get on with the business of relating their poems with confidence and clarity. Some poems have matter-of-fact delivery; some require a quieter mind.

Not all of the poems are of equal strength, but the eclectic mix shown here allows for that 'don't fence me in' sense to prevail through the rage-rage poems by Trish Casey as well as the sensual and clever poems by Maureen Gallagher. Betsy Carreyette will do her damnedest to make a better life for those four chirping daughters, while Susan Millar DuMars will not rush sadness, but instead make language do its poignant job of revealing and evoking strong feelings of what happens when someone we know and love is no longer with us. Her style of retelling is unique; she doesn't mince her words, she spares them and makes them work.

Pat Jourdan embraces a wider social scoop. Her characters ramble off to annoy 'the equal opportunities board'. She mingles with 'the friends of Icarus who fell off centre' in her poem 'Mayakovsky Roams Knocknacarra'. She tells us that 'land-grab machines mulch and overturn'. In 'His Strategy' her accountant 'red-ruled chaos into place'. If Pat Jourdan warns, then Caoilinn Hughes weaves. She weaves an exactness that makes you pay more attention to the sound, the music, and the song she puts before you. She has a remarkably mature way of seeing for someone so young.

The six different voices in this anthology never slump on energy and vision. Their commitment is to language and its flexibility. Their celebration and protest is as individual as each poem contained here. The quality of the voices adds to that intriguing journey of difference that makes you want more from all six.

Rita Ann Higgins
April 2004

Preface

A new anthology of poems by a relatively new publishing imprint is always a welcome thing, not least for the fact that it signals the commitment to and enthusiasm for poetry upon which especially new poets depend in order to exercise and develop their talents.

This new anthology of six Galway based women poets from Ainnir Publishing is therefore both an intriguing snapshot of what is going on in just one Irish city's poetry-making community, and also a reminder of how the geographical distribution of resources can help to marshal and organise a diverse group of individual writers into, effectively, a small movement for the visibility of good writing in their community. However private might be the journey of any one such a gathering is to turn the crossroads into a meeting place and the marketplace into a place of glimpsed or shared wonders.

Among the poets featured here, Betsy Carreyette is drawn to connections in and disparities of scale, from a consideration of the September 2001 attack on the World Trade Centre to poems of nature and the body in which 'zooming in' is an intrinsic part of her method of representation; Maureen Gallagher shows her ear for the tonal possibilities of words and, by concentrating in the main on single images, discovers the power of extended metaphor; Pat Jourdan makes poems that engage with politics, both with a large and a small 'p', and describes the all-too familiar sense of feeling, what one poems calls, 'Torn between the poem and the real'; Susan Millar DuMars combines an almost confessional honesty and intimacy with an eye for the telling, memorable detail; and, my personal favourite, Trish Casey, straining at the edges of lyric form, incorporates reported speech, elements of the cut-up technique, narrative asides, and a caustic eye for the fashionable contemporary in poems that are one minute laugh-out-loud, the next minute troubling and thought provoking.

Not all of the poems or indeed poets included here will please any given reader. The enthusiasm, common to most writers, to connect with even a modest public, can sometimes lead to the publication of work that might better have been left a little longer to mature. But as a further reminder that engaged and spirited poetry continues to be written throughout the country, this anthology, in casting a wide and generous net, will almost certainly be seen to have brought at least one or two very promising poets to the public's attention.

Pat Boran

Introduction By Todd Swift

I'm no stranger to anthologies. I have edited a few, and been in love with many. My first poetry book belonged to my mother, from her college days at McGill. It was blue, printed on near-onion paper, dog-eared, and every third line was furiously underlined in green or red ink. Words would be circled, in poems by e.g. Cummings, or my favourite, Kenneth Fearing. I must have been ten or eleven when this anthology broke my heart and seduced me all at once. Who can ever forget their first Dylan Thomas or Robert Frost poem? These brief lyric poems had the fragile, necessary intensity of the long icicles that hung outside my bedroom window, glowing in the moonlight. I enjoyed opening my window, and breaking them off in my hand, to bring in like luminous, fast-fading daggers. Poems would last longer.

My love of poetry, then, is synonymous with the anthology. Where others have found fault with these collections - for their arbitrary nature, their lack of depth, their provisional status - I have always revelled in their perfume of the manifesto, their fragmented nature, their air of being a secret whispered by an elite spy (who loves you): anthologies are flawed, dangerous rumours, printed and handed out like the gospels; they are a taboo dressed in their Sunday Best.

But most truthfully, they are the best way to find out what other people think is worth reading. There is so much poetry! Too much, I'd say, except I always want more. The idea of a new poet winning a prize out of the blue, or coming out with a first book, or placing a poem in a journal for the first time is like angels getting their wings in *A Wonderful Life:* saccharine yes, but ultimately a happy moment. The more new poets there are, the better chance we have to discover new varieties of the art, new worlds, new visions, and new styles. It also means one more reader for our own work (poets make the best readers). But I digress.

The fact that there is so much poetry 'out there' means no one can read it all. There has long been a familiar trope about poetry as a kind of terra incognito - we are always being told a particular poet or book 'maps new terrain' or helps set 'new bearings' - as if we were all in danger of falling down a hole, rather than stumbling across just another unexpectedly fine poet or poem. And so it is, that to keep the lawns trim and our lives if not bookshelves tidy, some British editors and critics pretend there is far too little good poetry, and that anthologies are like those well-farmed hedges that keep our neighbours pleasantly invisible. This is the Oxbridge way of coping with the wilderness - define it out of existence (witness a recent anthology by a famous Faber poet whose Introduction begins by explaining why only 35 poets in the UK are worth reading, and all of them comfortably 'Mainstream' - his term not mine).

But the true anthology, as I have suggested above, is a small shard of the polar ice-cap: its very presence gestures to, implies, the nine-tenths of a wild beyond still waiting to be explored. In other words, you either believe poetry is various, living, ever-evolving and deeply rewarding, like an Amazonian eco-system - or you see it as an English Garden, to be policed, over determined and kept within a green and pleasant margin, for fear it might accidentally come to resemble Nature, that thing it mirrors like the Thames pantomimes at being Niagara.

All of the anthologies I have edited or co-edited have been both deeply flawed, and very innovative, for the same reasons: they took risks, held their breath, and jumped. Into deep, always-moving waters. They were not frozen moments, snapshots only, but ice that shifts back to water, and runs away, warmed by a reader's reception. I am speaking here about process, community, praxis, and the creative act of making anthologies in the way film-makers make documenta-ries: one person, or event, at a time, edited into a contrapuntal abundant arc that tells many stories in a few reels. Take a clutch of good, different poets, put them 'together' in a book, and watch the contingent, the accidental, the random, flower into something valuable, risky, fun, maybe even life-changing.

So it is with the collection you have before you.

This is as far from being a 'global survey' - you'd think - as an anthology can get. It's pretty specific: women poets based in Galway, writing in the 21st century; and not even all that many "women poets" but, six. The kind of reader who is really a shopper might want bargains, and think they can find more 'content' elsewhere. Let me digress at this point, again, to bemoan the marketing of poetry now. Every blurb, every flyer, every announcement, every review, reads like a new deodorant, not poem, was up for grabs: we are promised the new, the sexy, the instantly gratifying, as if poetry (for instance) was not also about the very old, the gruesome, and the difficult. Back to the anthology at hand, which actually is pretty new and sexy. But it is more than that. It really is a microcosm. I think we're all familiar now with the fractal notion: that the curvaceous, troublingly non-linear shape or edge of a snowflake or a leaf manages to say something about the whole it is a part of. This is probably the best a poem can manage, too: to be so individual as to be 'universal', and so ideal as to be particular. More often, all poems fall to one side or the other. I've never seen the universality of some of, say, Armitage's laddish tones (because I don't like football nor feel the need to, like a politician, pretend to enjoy sports); nor does all of Blake, on the other extreme, win me over to his vision of Heaven and Hell. But between the too-provincial and the cumbersome grand yawp of some mystic-poets, occurs most poetry: it comes from one person, but the voice says a lot to a lot of people, if they'd only listen.

So too with a good anthology. It may seem rather limited in scope (universe in a grain of sand as the argument goes) but extend in many directions all at once. This collection does that, very well. For, the six women poets writing in Galway happen to offer a multitude of ways of being poets now. I won't lie and say all poetic options are present and accounted for (the avant-garde language school seems to be at home for the day with a stomach ache) but what we find here is still pretty impressive: from Jourdan's acerbic, satiric, powerful protests, to Gallagher's formalist slash free verse lyrics, to the younger spoken/word and slam champ heroics, we get the stages, from rock, to pop, to classical.

Galway is obviously a very good place to be a poet right now. It seems to have all the prerequisites: dedicated poets, editors, organizers, and support from the community, and the government; good festivals, readings, bookstores. It is developing into a place to go and live and write poetry. How else to explain the health this collection exhibits?

One thing that surprised me, though: the sadness, and the politics. For, in fact, while many of these poems are well-crafted, witty, and engaging, in the way critics want the above-mentioned Mainstream poems to be, there's another stream here: a serious, pained one. These poems mourn, grieve, decry. They protest. They warn. They promise revolution. For, the 21st century is also a terrible (in the Yeatsian sense) place to be a poet. See New York. See Iraq. See Madrid. See all the dead these poets know, and love. And the living they wish to protect. Galway, like the rest of the world, finds itself in this new century. So it is that poets thrive and struggle, all at once, with the ways and means to express the pain and joy. I'd say more, but we know too well how our lives fan out and spiral in, to take in the great tragedies, and the local victories - not just poets get to be that complex, we all do.

This is a good collection of poets to discover, some promising, some under-rated, many destined for better things. All worth reading or hearing. Open the window, reach out, and take hold of the glowing ice. It will unfold in your hand, and make the Thames look, well, tame. In comparison. Poetry is everywhere; especially, this instant, right here. Or a few pages away…
time to explore.

Todd Swift
London
March 15, 2004

Pat Jourdan

Anti Nazi Demo 1
Cinderalla Reconsiders...2
Culture..3
Details of the Marriage 4
Experience...5
Propaganda..7
Running Away 8
Survivors 9
Waiting for the Prince 10
War Sirens, Liverpool...11
A Good Area...12
His Strategy..13
Mayakovsky Roams Knochnacarra 14

Maureen Gallagher

Letting Go 17
The Seventeenth of March 2001 18
There's a Peach in the Fridge...19
No Strings...21
Spring 22
Confetti on a Grave...23
Tory Island...24
The Smell of April 25
Opportunity 26
Change...27

Trish Casey

Half of 29
Peter stays in Granny's House 30
To the Woman God said...31
Hmm?...32
Scenes from the City on Saturday Night 34
Midway...37
Lipstick Resistance..38

SUSAN MILLAR DuMARS

Shirt 41
Winter, Eggs 42
Home from Work 44
Open Palms 45
Fallen, 1973 48
Cathal, Briefly 49
Honey 50
Knowing About Your Life 51

BETSY CARREYETTE

Early Birds 53
Three Minute Silence 54
Day in the Life 56
Metamorphosis 57
Passage 58
Untitled 60

CAOILINN HUGHES

Upon a First Encounter 63
Crave 64
Before Dawn 66
The Crow 67
The Sound of War 68
Theatre Going 70

Pat Jourdan

Pat Jourdan was born in Liverpool, where she graduated from Liverpool College of Art. There have been several exhibitions of her paintings in London, Norwich, Dublin and Galway. She is divorced, with two sons. Her poetry has been published in The Shop, The Burning Bush, Poetry Ireland Review, The Rialto, Orbis and many more. Pat was previously published in 'Strictly Private', a Penguin anthology (edited by Roger McGough) and in 'The Common Thread' (Mandarin). She is winner of the Molly Keane Writing Award 2002 and the Cootehill Poetry Award 2002 and was broadcast on RTE's Rattlebag Poetry Slam and on Sunday Miscellany. She is editor of The Lantern Review. Her new collection of poetry, Turpentine,was published by Motet Press 2004, with a previous collection, The Bedsit, by Motet Press 2002.

Anti-Nazi Demo

Torn between the poem and the real,
our feet hurting in the cold
we pull down long jumble-sale sleeves
over our hands as imitation gloves.
Surrounding police do not complain,
in secret rooms they have been trained,
though their feet, too, grow cold.
Together in the dark
only the silver medallions
on their helmets gleam out -
they are a human railing.
These ones we know, local lads,
or some sent in from country towns,
broad Norfolk faces and round accents.
Words we have learned in history books
(first printed, reprinted and revised),
words which poets slam
into weak poems, to tart them up,
words like truth, democracy, devotion,
or dying words, like respect -
out here in the dark
we dance a gavotte with the police
with these words as tune.
Without words we are on a par with the thugs,
black leather's the same on any pair of shoulders.
Demo is a cheap way of spending an evening,
but to have stayed indoors
on this cold night
would have cost so much more.

Cinderella Reconsiders

These glass slippers hurt my feet.
At mealtimes I don't know which knife to use.
At night he's drinking claret with his pals -
I miss the kitchen and my mousy friends.
These salons lead through arches and colonnades,
chandeliers dripping rich cascades of light.
Where is my dull fat godmother?
-not with these painted courtiers,
their silken accents and brocaded clothes.
Ladies-in-waiting snigger when I speak.
My hands rest, useless, in my lap,
no water to draw, no coals to set,
my nails growing cruel and long.

Culture

On the way to school
I shall write a poem about Spring.
It will be about daffodils and crocuses.
Our daffodils emerged blind again
the soil was sour
and some dog crashed into our tulips.
An edge of sunlight spreads all down the road,
sides of cars collecting all the light -
Vauxhall, Fiesta, Ford
all fighting for their space.
Lorries pavement-parked
deliver sides of pigs into the butcher's
and this morning's mushrooms from the country
(somewhere in the phonebook.)
Dogshit litters everywhere,
I have to pay attention to each footstep,
can't gaze or dream into that distance
always blue, always beautiful
reaching into the ordinary street.
At school none of this will be mentioned,
nor the man who follows me back home,
his video-shot eyes uncovering me.

Details of the Marriage

Words I never knew before

the uses of love

(say you will)

mix into this catastrophic fall

(just one look)

has no mortgage

no bricks can surround it,

house-deeds or rent book or insurance ;

all false ; (forever and ever.)

Here the decree absolute

in my hands, a tissue screen,

through it I see

fluttering photographs

and a penalty clause.

Quickly shuffling the few cards left

(find the lady)

you name your price, the three-card trick,

a liquidation sale, all stock must clear.

In open court, before the judge,

the secrets of the marriage bleed out.

Experience

I am the witch that did not sink -
there has to be just one.
Oh, I tried to faint,
tried to scatter curses
but the men's hold was too strong,
their shrieks and shouts
drowned out my own.
Of course I sank,
billowing down into that glassy brown,
the brackish stream edging our village.
But I was borne upwards, like tides, like currents,
in water's blind delivery,
a new body from water and air.

Now I can mutter round the streets
while other women hide
they cannot stop me -
can feed my cats; let men visit late at night;
can exit after curfew;
wear skirt hems any length I choose.
My mind can feed on anything,
I am the witch that did not sink,
a bobbing apple saved by Eve
and as I strew the floor

with dank weeds, wet litter, cascades of green,
there is no guilt in my dark rank stink.

Now I can scutter round the streets
and clasp their arm
and utter truths, spew insights
(coughing out waterweeds,)
look at their face, intent.
Always they avoid my eyes,
shift focus, slide viewpoint,
afraid of what I might have learnt,
all of them too frightened to go
down to the river where it all begins,
the forced drinking-cup
of that reverse baptism.

Propaganda

First drops of blood came
one lunchtime at home
eating meat-pies, reading Enid Blyton.
The new secret stretched classroom walls.

The morning after her first encounter
with all that man can mean,
pavements scattered with broken diamonds
and she hid womb-deep a secret
that the world knew more about than her.

The instant that the baby shrieked
her skin slackened into emptiness,
body reshaped, breasts filled.

Yet here she appears,
bland image on glossy magazines
giving out an odalisque propaganda
that all should look like this
  - as if nothing had ever happened.

Running Away

Running away -
the thing I do best
collecting a year and its clothes
[dashing off]
strewing photographs along pavements
as I go
[oh, keep me, keep me,]
somewhere in the routine of your prayers,
the silly doorstep rituals,
flittering calendar pages, cups of tea.

When the air changes shape and smell,
springtime prowling up backstreets
I am still there
playing out in that sunset,
our gang before bedtime,
ollies in the dry gutters.
[Keep me, keep me]
I have to hurt you
like all driven animals
running, running
away from food and water.
Oh how we fear safety.
Let us run.
[Keep us]
Let us run.
[Stay behind]
Let us go,
the blue "away" is the only place we belong.
I run impeccably - I have skill in this.

Survivors

We are the friends of Icarus,
who fell off-centre
beyond the painting's edge;
no poet saved us.

We gulped and struggled in dirty seas-
no-one noticed; the ships sailed on.
Seaweed-strewn we straggled to the shore.
No-one arrived. We stank.
At city's edge we took new names,
ones they'd understand, hid
the visions, hallucinations and tests,
weeks dashing to and fro the camel's eye.
We know what happens off-scene,
the shabby survival,
cards with a marked corner
and in our rented rooms
we keep new wings, freshly laundered,
sequin-bright, stacked, waiting.

Waiting for the Prince

The seven persons of restricted growth
have gone off to annoy
the equal opportunities board.
The vermin-control agent
has exterminated all the mice.
European regulations have imposed
an import quota on pumpkins
and pollution, over-development,
acid seepage and a virus
have killed off all the frogs.
Glass slippers contravene the trades description act.
Cancelled, the palace ball did not acquire
the requisite singing-and-dancing licence
nor permission to consume liquor on palace premises.
The Prince's agent has been unmasked,
a part-time human trafficker and pimp,
deceiving young girls with outlandish promises.
Transformed by botox and cosmetic surgery
the two Ugly sisters are cover-girls
with a new song climbing the charts.
The Fairy Godmother, retrained in computers,
runs a new Women's Opportunities course;
the castle converted into flats, the baron divorced,
it's a new panto entirely,
and with Aids about, sex is unmentionable again.
Snow White and Cinderella have fallen for the same man;
the Prince is in hiding.

War Sirens, Liverpool

An orange sky dancing with light -
she holds me up to see more -
"St Luke's is on fire!"
The adults are afraid, I feel them
shift the dread from one
to another. I watch the sparks.
The church's black shape persists,
held up by traceries, fanlights,
delicate stonework containing
the dashing explosions.
Skies are not orange
nor churches alight;
wartime tip-tilts all city rules,
adults adrift in fear.

Gone. Green lawns disguise
inside-and-outside surviving walls.
The church stands shocked,
a circlet of burnt stone.

Any siren brings it back,
that churning in the gut,
wires of veins alert,
the unrunning of no escape.
Memory buries everything,
attempts to smother a burning church.

A Good Area

Why should they need a passport?
Where should they go? It is nice here,
like sinking into a watercolour
(Still Life with flowers and kittens.)
Nothing to fight or die for,
everything nice.
Trips to the country spread suburban certainty.
Emotions recollected safely,
never in full spate, raw, now.
Lots of trees.
Relatives play bitparts when necessary.
No politics.

The poems reek of central heating,
middlebrow religion
and a bit of the picturesque,
dull prisms, one side blank.
Oh no, dustbinmen do not invade this poem,
their reckless spillage,
their dawn-raid fatigue.

His Strategy

With accountant's trim lines
he red-ruled chaos into place.
A rhyming dictionary in his desk –
yet when the house was cleared
the rhymes had gone,
all fell slackly into prose
meandering into another home.
Auctioneers carted the desk away.
Investments pinioned tight
the lilting rhyme.

Mayakovsky Roams Knocknacarra

("Clouds have trousers" – Vladimir Mayakovsky)

It was easy then to dash about the fields
passing the sharp bends of the stone walls,
my eyes casting about those fields' rough shapes,
treading their unevenness
as I chanted and shouted and pleaded.
Sometimes it WAS work, getting the quota right –
other times it was worse,
the trails of my townlands
to be proclaimed and mourned and raged at.

Now each field is sundered by houses,
land-grab machines mulch and overturn.
All is made straight, trim and tarred,
pounded to conform.
Roads spread like arcade-games
from barren roundabouts.
Even the clouds have trousers.
If I shout in the streets
they put me in the unit;
if I protest at the developers
they put me in the cells.
From Russia to Knocknacarra is the same,
a poet is dangerous, is despised.

Later they name a road in my honour.

Maureen Gallagher

Maureen Gallagher was born in Monaghan. At present she lives in Galway where she works as a special needs resource teacher. She began writing poetry in 1998. Since then her work has appeared widely in Ireland, Britain, Canada, The United States and New Zealand in The Shop, Poetry Ireland Review, West 47, Orbis, The Rialto, Envoi, The Reater, Poetry Nottingham International, The Journal, Iota, Psychopoetica, Poetry Monthly,  *Connections, Weyfarers, The Coffee House, Pulsar, The Interpreter◊s House, Potpourri (US), Free Lunch (US), The Laire (US), The Leading Edge(US), Pottersfield Portfolio (US), River King Poetry Supplement (US) and others.*

Maureen also writes prose and her short stories have appeared in The Sunday Tribune, Staple (Issue 59), The Frogmore Papers (forthcoming), Books Ireland, Ropes and West 47. She has had reviews and criticism published in The Cork Literary Review, Staple 58, Ropes, The Burning Bush, The Connaught Tribune among others. She was a prizewinner in the 'New Writer 2002' essay competition. Maureen has given readings of her poetry many times at poetry events including at Galway Arts Centre, the Western Writers' Centre, University College Galway and the Project Arts Centre. In June 2002, she was a finalist in the Dublin Writers' Festival Poetry Slam. Her work has been broadcast on RTE's Rattlebag. Maureen has been selected for the Poetry Ireland Introductions readings in 2004.

Letting Go

He's very wise, my man.
He doesn't try to build on sand.

Nor does he get upset
when rain is wet
or the sun hot,
for what,
as he says himself,
is the point?

What I'd like to know is,
how do you become wise?
How do you learn
to let go?

He lets go.

Being wise, he knows
no-one ever goes
away.

Even when you die, he says,
warming to the subject now,
you re-appear in time
as molecules,
in the air.

Not too well up on molecules,
but fascinated all the same, I say,
in that case,
if *you* died,
couldn't I breathe you in?
We'd really be together, then.
Forever.

Not very wise, he says.

The Seventeenth of March 2001

There's a germ invading the air
as invisible as Banquo's ghost,
searching for a hoof or a jaw
to clamp on: parades are off.

The Nasdaq index is plunging,
flailing like a bungee jumper
with a death wish; the tortured punter
reflects on a future of ruin.

Marinated in gin, the Titan,
who once ran a marathon, declining,
is addicted to a different accounting
and daily slides further than the Dow.

Winter's in howling retreat,
temperatures slip by degrees,
it's the seventeenth of March 2001,
spring cherries are risking defeat.

hoof & jaw - foot & mouth

There's a Peach in the Fridge

There's a peach in the fridge
you have it.

But please
take your time:
peaches are
unsatisfying
when cold.

First,
feather-
touch
the whole
fruit.

Now lick it.

Feel the fur
as it yields,
as it gives,
as you tongue

the flesh swelling
to meet your mouth,
the juice oozing
between your teeth.

Some people
eat peaches
too quickly.
They seize them,

squeeze them,
gobble them down
too fast,
too soon,
no good.
What's the rush?

Take it *easy*.

Anticipation whets
the appetite.
Take your *time*.

Alright!

Now !

Now!

YES!

And appreciate please,
I do not offer peaches
to just anyone these days.

No Strings

I was your whole book back then:
you devoured me.

Your window to a new world,
with a word on everything,
I encouraged you
to write your own world.

You did that
but ended up
with more characters
than space.

So you cut me down:
from chapter to paragraph,
to sentence,
to, finally,
full stop.

Then, being modern,
you dispensed with punctuation altogether.

Spring

It's been a year since we met in Java's Café,
since you sent that Kandinsky 'with love';
the world's been slipping into slump since:
things look set to get worse. It's Spring.

Politically the focus is fertility: cell division,
implantation, the issue of the right
to choose or not. It feels like winter
though the birds keep mentioning March;

an icy wind still blows
whipping notices off poles
except those immovable posters
reproaching self-destructive imposters.

Daffodils assert the primacy of bright
yellow; snowdrops the wonder of white;
the birds are right: it's time to think
of light and sun, the advance from

amoeba to man, nature to culture:
the primordial to the Rites Of Spring
and Improvisation Twelve - Kandinsky,
from nucleus-dividing life to love.

The Rites Of Spring - Stravinsky symphony

Improvisation Twelve - Kandinsky painting

Confetti on a Grave

I gave you a last gift - a rose,
pale petals you casually plucked
and watched indifferently fall,
like confetti on a grave.

Custom dictates black for the passing away
when white might be more appropriate;
death is often the best solution:
why not rejoice the demise
of an item that's done?
Bury it deep
so no trace of it remains.

That's not a rose I toss on the turf,
but the chador you wove, to shroud growth,
hidden in a grim cave, shrivelling.

Personally, I prefer crimson
for an occasion like this.
In any case, from now on,
colour will be worn,
from indigo to green;
I've done with mourning,
it's time to 'unweave the rainbow'.

Tory Island

No seabirds to be seen, only gulls;
we'd missed the puffins with their exotic beaks,
their nesting time - June - long over;
instead we looked at the ridge and

wondered how many aeons since
the cliff face tilted. Was it an ice age
or continental drift? Imagine,
once we could have walked to America -

what a boon that would have been
for famine relief! But time divides
events and space; nature has a habit
of making us feel infinitely small.

We scrutinised the layers of sediment
for fossils, ruminating on parallels
with human development; early dreams,
calcified in the gravity of existence,

no longer fit the characters we've become;
like petrified trilobites, anachronistic,
redundant - except as a curiosity, a tribute
to what we once were - they no longer apply.

The Smell Of April

the aroma of coconut whin
arousing spring

the tang of forbidden sex
on a guilty afternoon

tiger lilies sneezing
in the homes of the nouveau riche

a suspicion of cat's pee
from basil planted on sills

from satellite to small screen
the choking charred buildings

the infectious fetor of fear
rummaging through rubble in Jenin

Opportunity

Hormones in the air
sabotage the briefings
at the induction course
to improve resource teaching:
hens plump feathers;
a lone cock crows.

One of the females,
affecting disdain,
her focus on testing
to buck the testosterone
that sucks her in,
succumbing,

notes the raven plumage,
with a pepper of pearl;
parted in the middle. Tall.
Resembling.

A chance encounter.
Dissembling.

He flirts. She fantasises.
Nothing between them
but colliding molecules.
And opportunity.

Change

No one called. The blank red eye gapes back at me:
an unblinking stare. My days lack necessity,
as shapeless as old pyjamas whose elastic has
lost all tension, my life down around my ankles.

Where all the urgent calls: contacts to make,
articles to write, meetings attend?
The question hangs like a dustcover in a space
once occupied by camaraderie.

You don't dip your toe in the same stream
twice. Water converts to ice when temperature
drops. Nothing remains as before.
Such qualitative change impossible to ignore.

Trish Casey

Winner of the Best Performance Prize in the RTE Rattlebag Slam at Dublin Writers' Festival 2003. Selected for this year's Poetry Ireland Introductions Series.
"...a wonderful poet..." Annie Proulx, Pulitzer Prize Winner. "...blow to the solar plexus." The Irish Times. "...the perfect poet for our dark era - funny, aggressive, tender, insightful, confrontational ... If Lenny Bruce were reincarnated as a feisty Irish woman, he'd strut the stage as Trish Casey." Ken Bruen, Crime Novelist.

Trish Casey, from the harbour town of Cobh in Co. Cork, is a graduate of the Gaiety School of Acting. She also voice-trained with the IORC Academy, Cork, and at Walton's School of Music, Dublin. Trish writes and performs poetry, short monologues and dramatic works on interpersonal, social and political themes. Her performances incorporate movement, chanting, singing, ritual and the use of props.

Trish has performed her work at the Sirius Arts Centre, Cobh, alongside Annie Proulx; Galway City Library in the "On the Edge" series 2003, Clifden Community Arts Week 2003, Nimmo's Restaurant for the Bretagne Festival 2003, as well as the Town Hall Studio and Scribbler's Wine Bar, Galway; the Bank of Ireland Arts Centre, Dublin, for the Business to Arts Showcase 2002 and in the "Out to Lunch" series 2003; Triskel Arts Centre, Cork, for Art Trail 2002, the CAT Club, Kinsale Arts Festival, Cork Midsummer Arts Festival, Éigse na gCúige, the Munster Literature Centre, Cork; and the Dylan Thomas Centre, Swansea, as part of the Cork/Swansea Cultural Exchange 1997.

Half Of

No, see Cindy is my half of a sister and Luke is my half of a brother.
Cindy and Luke and the Blonde Bitch live down town with Daddy.
I live here with Mammy and Charlie.
Charlie's funny.
Daniel and Derek stay with us sometimes.
Charlie's their Dad. They're not half-ofs.
I hate them anyway - they're always fighting and they tear the wallpaper.

Mammy wants Charlie to be my Dad. I don't -
I have a Dad, and I wouldn't want another one.
If Charlie became my Dad, Daniel and Derek wouldn't be half-ofs -
They'd be steps Mammy says. Well I don't want steps like them -
They scare our cat Sissie and throw stones at Mr Murphy's dog.
I don't want steps. I have half-ofs -
I love Cindy and Luke.

I'd like it to be Cindy and Luke and Daddy and me.
Then Charlie couldn't try to be my Father.
I wish the Blonde Bitch would go back to where she came from -
Like Mammy says -
So I could live with Daddy.
If Mammy got rid of Charlie and Daddy got rid of the blonde bitch,
Then Daddy and Mammy and me could live together.

But then the Blonde Bitch would take Cindy and Luke away,
Coz she owns them. But Daddy half owns them as well.
I'd cry if Cindy and Luke went away -
So I suppose it's better if we all stay where we are.
Granny says it's an awful fuckin' mess -
But she says I'm never to say "fuckin'" -
But I think it's an awful fuckin' mess too.

Peter stays in Granny's House

We place a two-week-old newspaper
on the kitchen table.
With a pen,
he marks out the fins
for his Killer Whale Suit -
a black bin-bag
with a white plastic hanger
for a tail,
lying on the hall floor.
He brings his pen
round a small heading
near the end of the page:

Belgian Police Arrest Man for Serial Killings

"Finished, now will you cut them out for me?
And it's okay if you go outside the line."

... severed body parts of up to six women ...

"Where is Granny's Sellotape for to stick them on?"

... hands, feet, arms ...

"See, we still need something that looks like a whale's head."

... thighs ... a torso ... in 15 bin-bags ...

He climbs into the whale suit
and I cover his head
with the black fabric I've found
in the old clothes box.
He lies still,
waiting for Granny
to come from the sitting-room
to guess what he is.

To the woman God said:

I shall give you intense pain in childbearing,
you will give birth to your children in pain.
Your yearning will be for your husband,
and he will dominate you.

Genesis 3:16

Adam's Apple

S e x y
    married her

she made
    noisy babies

    went flabby
        killed her
            got a good deal
        on a
            wife scrapage scheme
        sold her
            noisy babies

Evesong

To God the woman said:

The serpent he is dead -
I **ate** him
after the apple.

And as for you -
OMNI-POTENT MONOLITH
of the
DEIFIED PHALLUS -

get to hell out of my garden
or I just might **eat**
you
as well.

Hmm?

She lies on a bed in a cubicle in Casualty,
a nurse checking her pulse.
"Susan ...
Joyce, isn't it?"
"Yeah."
"So Susan,
what possessed you to try this then,
hmm?"

Susan assumes that's a rhetorical question.
Nurse...
Stanton
hardly cares to hear the hackneyed tale
of an alcoholic rapist
for a father
and a near catatonic heap
for a mother.
Nurse Stanton is hardly interested
in the details
of a trip to England for an abortion.
She hardly wants to know
the specifics
of a previous hospitalisation
for an eating disorder.
Nurse Stanton hardly cares to hear the truth at all,
does she now,
hmm?
"Well…
I wanted to go away for the weekend
but I had no money,

so I decided to take an overdose instead."
"I'd advise you not to be so smart, missy.
We'll have to pump you out.
It's a nasty procedure.
Do you want me to contact anyone for you?"

A doctor emerges, clipboard in hand, from
behind the drawn curtain.
"Susan ...
Joyce, isn't it?
So Susan,
what was the purpose of all this then,
hmm?"
"Dr J....
Kingston, isn't it?
So, Dr Kingston,
take a flying fuck, why don't you,
hmm?"

Scenes from the City on Saturday Night

I
He arrives. They play music. They laugh. They get drunk.
They argue. He beats her.
She cries. They make up. They have sex. They eat pizza.

II
The redhead vomits on her silver platforms,
exposing her black silk knickers
as her short slip skirt slides up her bare thighs.

III
He staggers.
He trips.
He loses his grip.
A speeding ambulance squashes his chips.

IV
she snorts a line

o r   t w o

o r   t h r e e

an' wears the redclingy-allcleavage number
an' finds a willing feckless male

V
Your man in the Levis and the Nike Air Max
breaks a bottle against a down-pipe
and lunges at the guy in the Umbro sweatshirt.

VI
She exudes that "screw me" sex appeal.
He hands her a drink.
He checks his reflection.
He straddles his stool.

VII
foot to the floor
adrenaline score
yeah

the squad in pursuit   neenaa
neenaa neenaa
the boys   the boys
                              b u z z i n'

VIII
Semicomatose in some stranger's car,
divested of thong and Wonderbra.

IX
He lies on a trolley in a corridor in Casualty,
a nurse checking his pulse.

X
Shop window -
SMASH IT.
Phone booth -
WRECK IT.
"The fuzz is comin'!"
"Fuck it!"
"Leg it!"

XI
Foul taste on tongue
smoke-ensnared hair
faded after-shave on tired thighs.

XII
fast-food wrappings
shattered glass

empty condom packet

rivulets of pavement piss
pool of blood

random vomit

CHEERS

Midway

They offer garlands to the ocean
in honour of the bravest.
Over cups of tea
talk of heroes -
Veterans
in search of sunken vessels -
Former enemies -
A wave of memories -
Both sides told
through old men's tears.

Lipstick Resistance
(For Peg Amison)

Afghanistan, reign of the Taliban, 2001:
Palette of eyeshadow on a dresser;
Eyeliner, blusher,
Lipstick -
The arsenal of anarchists.
They move through the streets -
Mute
Lip-loud anarchists,
Shrouded in baby-blue burqas.

Bergen-Belsen liberation, 1945:
Survivor supplies arrive -
Food, clothes, medicine,
And mysteriously,
Lipstick.
Branded with a serial number;
Brutalised, demonised, subjugated;
They paint cracked lips
And seal their claim -
First precious piece of self
Regained.

Susan Millar DuMars

Susan Millar DuMars was born in Philadelphia in 1966. She moved to Ireland in 1998. In between these times she earned a BA from Hampshire College in Massachusetts; and an MA in Writing from the University of San Francisco. Her poetry, fiction and non-fiction have appeared in magazines in the UK, US and Ireland. She edits fiction for Ainnir Publishing, and poetry for the Poets Against the War website. She is the co-organiser of the  *Over the Edge reading series in Galway, where she also teaches creative writing.*

Susan's poetry has previously appeared in the following publications: Oxygen (US), Nth Position website, The Burning Bush (Ireland), The Galway Advertiser, Earth's Daughters (US), Arrowsmith (US), Poetry Motel (US), On San Francisco, Crannóg, Gateway Poetry Anthology (US). "Shirt" was a finalist in the Rattlebag/Dublin Writers' Festival Poetry Slam of 2003, and was broadcast on RTE One radio. Susan has been shortlisted for the Fish 2004 short story competition and is nominated for the 2004 Cúirt New Writing Prize.

Shirt

A silken splurge.
The color of loyalty,
Shade of serenity;
Summer sky blue.
It glides
Over the pouting
Flesh of his arms.
Floats
Into place across
The gassy globe of his belly.
He's ready.
Sucks in his gut as he
Steps out the door onto
Chestnut Street.
The yellow dust
Of civilization.
Traffic's savage music, the cruel
Flash of sun stroked metal,
A thousand shuffling feet.
His shirt protects him
From the siege of stares.
From the panting subway grate,
The bony billboard model,
The exhaust.
He feels almost safe;
Bravely, belly first, he meets
The heat-soaked day.

Winter, Eggs

I thought of Denice
In the deli section of Atkin's Market
Because she used to work there
(I saw her, for an instant,
under the fluorescents, in that stupid red
apron Mr. Atkins made her wear.)
And I thought, don't forget to call her,
and did I remember the eggs?

Walking uphill, into the wind,
hugging the groceries, scarred
and shrivelled apples from the orchard
underfoot. I'm trying to name the song
that was on the Muzak.
Thinking also of an omelette
and a strong cup of coffee.
A winter lunch.

Gretchen is waiting at the top of the driveway
Too pale, not waving, hugging her body
Where is her coat?
When I reach her she tells me,
"Put down the groceries,"
so I balance them on the hood of a car.
"- something to tell you. Denice -"
Call her. Eggs. Got them.
"- was on that plane. That we saw
on the news."
Explosion.

Grass on fire.
Seatbelts hanging from trees.
The groceries start to slide.
Gretchen steadies them.
My voice is like ice creaking
and shattering under our feet.

I remember
The song on the Muzak was "Fire and Rain"
And I saw her, for an instant
Her brown arms on the counter
Giggling with me about Hank Armstrong
Asking if I wanted to go swimming
at the reservoir, when she got off work
But that was summer.
We are deep in winter now.
The reservoir is silent, choked with ice.
I remembered the eggs, and I came home
And next I would have called her.

We head inside. Gretchen carries
the groceries.
Later, she puts them away.
Snowy white eggs, whole and perfect.
Safely away in the refrigerator.

Home from Work

The red rug floats like a postcard
on the cold lake of linoleum.
Mocking beard of dust
on the typewriter cover.
Unread post, unread papers.
Heartbeat blink of answering machine;
worlds and voices and questions, caged
on a toy sized tape.
Kitchenette:
a garlic bulb baker,
and a martini shaker, and the
single, veiny blue bowl bought at Pier One.
Oily cartons on the counter still smell
of plum sauce.
In the fridge, food hardening and curling
at the edges,
and gin, and olives, and always ice.
Neighbours' argument echoes
down the heating duct. A door slams,
a name is called, twice.
Chrome table legs capture last light.
Bedroom:
television clicked on,
like a fire in a cave.
Over the bed, tin Christmas angels.
All year round.
Canned laughter. That perfect sized hollow
in the mattress. That perfect first sip.
Darkness comes. Digital clock,
red numbers watching.

Floating on the cold lake.

Open Palms

i.
I dream of my dead
daughter.
I find her
buried under the cradling
roots of the maple tree-
silver skinned, flat boned
coiled and shuddering
in troubled sleep.
Salvageable.
With my hands
I excavate her.

Tilt the face
(a cold sliver of moon)
and breathe pink breath
into silver.
I wait
for her
unfolding,
her startled birth cry.

The man beside me
does not help me.
Instead,
like a bather testing the warmth of his bath,
he dips his toe into the dirt.
Then, with his soft palms,
pats a blanket of soil
in place over his shoes.
"How would it feel to be dead?" he muses.
"How would it feel-", as stars lurch
 and rain down like daggers,
"How would it feel to be-"

ii.
He holds his newspaper like a shield,
half lowered.
I sit beside him,
avoiding the flickering heat
of his eyes,
losing myself again
in the mane of his hair, copper-gold,
maple leaves in the last warm light
of an Autumn afternoon.
I am not well.
I'm breathing too fast,
and my hands can't seem to close
around anything.
Pencils and spoons
and house keys drop away
from my aching open fingers.
Facts and hard won insights slip away,
beyond my grasp.

I want him
to wake me from my troubled sleep.
To press his soft, open palms
to my face, as he did once,
when checking me for fever.
I want him to find me.

But his smile eats all the oxygen in the room,
and I am strangled blue
by the time he tells me
that everyone loves me.

iii.
I dream he is murdered.
The yard is scarred
with the boot prints of soldiers,
deep and sharp.
In the tall grass I find the head
of our German Shepard, still
faithfully watching.

A purple wailing echoes
inside the house.
Skulls shriek in the air–
and he is there,
alone and moaning,
poisoned, gassed,
blue and dying.
He does not know why.
His soft palms fall open
to the rain of stars.
The shrieking choir is silenced.
He is still
faithfully watching...

A child rises
from his body.
She is my daughter,
a silver vapour,
the last shadow he casts.
And she is smiling.
"I miss him," I tell her,
and in her father's soft, rusted voice, she says,
"I'm right here."

Fallen, 1973

Jesus - a snappy dresser
in cranberry velvet, butterfly sleeves,
Breck girl hair.
And I dress up for Him.
The navy coat with gold buttons
that waits all week,
sighing. I'm seven
and still chew my hair.
I make the world
with each click
of my black buckle shoes.

Sunday school - my chair rears up on its
hind legs, a stallion I am
taming. I'm good with wild things,
patient, fearless. Repeat :

Now I lay me down to sleep,
I pray the Lord my soul to keep...
(But death is a nothing, a nonsense word;
my life a party that no one ever leaves...)

Falling is like waking up.
The strings are cut.
My teacher lifts me from the floor,
rights my chair.
I cry because
No one caught me.
Nothing held me there.

Cathal, Briefly

The last time
I saw you
I said we were like
two old soldiers.
You smiled
with your whole face.

If I had known
your war was over;
that you had said,
Enough.

If I had seen
in your white smile
the ragged flag
of surrender…

But the last time
I saw you
I was glib,
useless.
Met Cathal, briefly
I wrote in my journal.
The last time.

Honey

I fold myself small as a postage stamp.
I crawl under the table.
I hide from the sky
I hide from eyes
I hide from everything
that will take me away.

Mother spreads honey on bread.
She is singing.
I stare at her knees,
large ruddy circles.
Mom, sing that song for me.
Don't let me leave you.
Keep me inside
your warm yellow kitchen.

I am invisible
but when she is finished
she passes the honeyed bread
to my cupped fingers
in the shadows
between the cold silver legs.

Mom, keep singing.
I am your daughter.

Knowing About Your Life

Sky multiplied by two
And thousands of hands

I told you I was leaving my body for a while,
and would you keep an eye on it while I was gone?

Black women dance in bright Sunday hats.
Wind chimes, jasmine. Safe.

The beating, the white spray

The palm trees made you sad ; like us,
they'd been transplanted.
I miss knowing about your life.

Soy mochas. Everyone in black,
no one in a hurry. Tim's red jeep. The bay.
Red wine jewel bright. Sinking through the afternoon.
This city is ours.

Sudden turn

Virginia Woolf's diaries, water pistol fish.
Crusty bread dripping with anchovies.
A tiny violin for the Christmas tree.

Sudden turn, sky

multiplied by two. The beating,
the white spray.
The ocean is here.
Here, too.

I miss knowing about your life.

Betsy Carreyette

Betsy Carreyette grew up in Scotland, but has lived in Galway for several years now. She has four daughters. Her poems have been published in West 47, The Burning Bush, Crannóg, The Lantern Review and others. She is a member of The Bridge Mills Writers' Group and was an On The Edge featured reader in May 2003.

Early Birds.

Morning's wings span the mountain
breaking the night
into a million pink skies.

Chirping daughters flock the kitchen
pouring bran flakes
into hand painted bowls

pushing copy books
in tatty school bags
shattering the silence in their squall

over Tupperware boxes
crinkling crisps
and who has the shiniest plums.

Three Minute Silence

When the twin towers were crucified
the thousands within locked
in terror
and all hell
looked set to break loose
Lyric fm played Gorecki's third symphony
and the US banned, 'Imagine'
though how fervently we imagined, beyond
the endlessly extended news bulletins
never up to date enough for our glut
with their views and juxtapositions of views
reels of screaming footage and newsprint enough
to smother the world.

Over pints we thirsted explanation, pointing
the finger
praying for peace, or revenge
or for the democratic union of America
or the death of all Arab nations
taking time out from work or school to summon
whatever God or Goddess we could muster
making a circle on the floor for the three min silence
four daughters and I each
lighting a candle
removing wax from the baby's mouth
hushing her with breast
during a fumbled explanation

that the world they are inheriting is really very fucked up
and there is no point pretending everything's rosy
when it so obviously isn't
and though we live in times of digital this, mobile that
the ability to email Timbuktu at the press of a button
how hard it is to sit down and discuss
who took whose pen, from whose bedroom.

Do not expect a civilised explanation neatly packed
for there is nothing civilised in this
hauling home of harvest
through the parted crowd
its twisting masquerade of venerated leaders
adhered so fast
to gilt faced books
cannot turn in the fanatical seat of their pants;
Yet above it all
 you shall rise
for I vowed to give you flight
the first time I took each
of your, slippery, warm
blood smeared bodies into my arms.
As intoxicated on the smell of birth -
as the Afghan mother beneath her burqa
the Cherokee mother in her reserve
or the mothers in New York City
who lay crushed beneath the debris
as we crouch here
on this toy strewn floor.....

Day in the Life

She couldn't face college.
All that 'smarten yersel up' shite;
Reception;
Her shaved hair;
Waitress uniform she wouldn't be seen dead in -
scratchy formless nylon thing
sending electric shocks through her body
with the move of every muscle;
The syrup-y smile of the other students
with their package holidays and pharmaceutical shares.

Disembarked at the shopping mall
rifling through sale price knickers,
whiling away hours over a mug of tea
before stalking her future through this
previously blitzed, Clydeside town
where concrete towers and crack cocaine
were the new order of the day;

Redundant of their shipyard,
it's workers hung out of bookies doorways,
pubs on the day the brew came through,
eyeballing any scowling young woman who might cross
their path.

Hours to spend before making the endless bus journey home
to deliver the latest progress report
in catering, and hotel management.

('brew': colloquialism for welfare payment.)

Metamorphosis

Something in the way you laid
a trail of broken biscuits across the beach
to divert that straggling peacock -

Zooming in on me again
with your sepia lens
on the most colourful day of the summer.

The sweltering sun spinning through a haze
induced by too much red wine
and too little sleep,
declared us larger than life
and penetrated, the depths of night
where alone I churned in a single bed.

Lolling myself before you -
while you grinned on cucumber cool
with your incredible smile.
Pausing for a breather during our 3 day conversation
when all seemed the preordained twinning of souls
'neath the water cascade of my minds eye
we baptised our bodies
and launched our minds.

Then home in a daze I wore
like a long black cloak
dripping river,
metamorphosing with my every step,
neither walking
nor flying
but somewhere between…

Passage

Come through the passage towards light
feel your body move through my own
on this journey of flesh
bringing us at last face to face.
Feel the hearty muscles of my vagina
grin wide in greeting
your shiny wet body venturing forth.
Listen to the language that sanctifies your skin
in ancient knowledge.
I am ready today
as I was that night last summer
beneath the stars
I am ready
to open wide
petal by ruby petal.

Untitled

Mother, years I have carried forth these seeds
ripening surely on harvest's turbulent wind
through this storm
I have come
stretching wide the heaving sky
in the crowning of a new sun.

Oceans have parted before me
I have been embraced in softest of arms
at every port of call;
I have lain beneath ocean
I have lain amid stars
I have lain naked with the best of men.
Mother, I have loved long and hard
devoted on the trail of scorching hooves.

Mother, you dark and silent horse
drifting in shadow
spinning in light;
I have slain men in your name.
Some of them kings.
I have no regrets.
I would do it again.

I have wielded the blade of my anger
with such precision
the sky gapes apart in wonder
as severed heads of grotesque gods
fall with all their bloody gore
into my sodden lap. Mother, on bended knees

I reach across your knowing dark body
flinging aside these fallen false prophets
by golden lengths of hair,
I have to clear the debris.

With the frenzied freefall of ramshackle religion
whose glorification is truly spent
tumbling to wretched feet
I have seen
whole empires;
Conspiracies;
Corrupt bureaucracies
whose flaming thirst raged higher and higher
find what it means
to burn out
of control.

I have heard history falter for breath
and sink into the dirt;
I have seen the lies it told glisten and spin
like silver winged birds into the open sky of illusion
and drop lifeless
into the ocean
like a stone

and I have lived to tell the tale.
Mother, I live to tell the tale.

Caoilinn Hughes

Caoilinn Hughes is a young writer from Galway.
She has been published in myriad journals and
anthologies in Ireland, the UK and U.S., such as;
The Shop, Poetry Now, West 47, Poetry.com
(anthologies), Westword, P.O.W., and many more.
She was runner up in the "Foyle Young Poet of the
Year Award 2002" and the "Western People Literary
Awards" in 2001. She read at monthly Poetry Slams
in the Cellar Bar, Galway for three years, which
included taking part in the yearly "International Poetry Slam Showcases"
for 2001, 2002, and 2003. She also read as an invited reader in the Galway
City Library in 2003 for the Western Writers Centres' "On the Edge" poet-
ry readings and again in January for the anniversary readings. She is cur-
rently undertaking a Joint Honours Degree in English and Drama at
Queen's University, Belfast.

Upon a First Encounter

A.M., and half past one,
Still you sit with hands
Clenched to clover, lemon,
And thick whiskey in crystal.

Here! One hundred euro and ten cent
For sense of a single thought of yours?
No? Silence. Just whiskey and the tick
Of a clock between us.

Dogs breathe behind us, heaving,
And any second now, will ambush to kill
A cricket whose ears are pinned
For little secrets you let to me.

Outside it's cold and black, a summer night
Stormy as October in the countryside.
Little paws rasp and steal your mind, again,
Hot whiskey, fast, warms inside.

A.M., and now it's two,
All this tonight will brew in me,
Stories shared between us two,
Empty bottle, glasses clink,
Lulled, dumbfound, now
Time to sleep…

Crave

For Sarah Kane

There, in my wishes, is ease-
My thoughts are chained
Step, speak, e-motion into a boundary.
Freedom could be a bodiless soul
Whose only earthliness is hope.
Call me if you're free.

I love the touch of skin,
Skin against numb skin,
Woman against man,
Black against white,
Flesh against warm bone
Call me if you'll touch me.

I crave, need always to crave.
Hold me. Hug me. Hit me.
Harder. Bruise me mentally.
Make me bleed and feel
And long to bleed and feel.
Call me when you crave.

I undress alone, know nothing,
Let down ego and machinery,
Imagine something else.
I switch. Down. Die. Gone.
Elucidating shadows.
Call me if you would Undress.

I hate to measure. Sagacity.

Don't answer me. Ask me.
Don't see me. Sense me.
Taste me, touch me, take me,
Save me. Transcend me and these conditions.
Call me, but I will not answer.

Before Dawn

The air whispers quietly
Words fit for poetry, tonight.
The orange lights glows soft as skin,
Gleaming sex onto a navy knight.
Who gallops by, and suddenly,
It is first light.
All the while I write, sitting
By the sill with the raw, frosty breeze
Keeping me awake and tight,
As the fog grows from fields
And the beams of light through
White clouds become everything
That matters now.
There are no people. No sounds.
Not a stir. I am alone
With this pink light knowing everything.
Mild, tranquil, simple, found.
And, I leave the sill, and the
Spry morning, and I leave my quill,
And as I turn my back, I know
That the sun will shoot into the sky,
And the birds in song will all arrive,
Both trees and weeds will come alive,
But I have seen the light at dawn,
And as it ends and day begins
It whispers soft goodnight.

The Crow

Amongst the limp branches,
The pale, sick leaves- swooping,
Drooping, caressing envious grass,
He hides.
His strong legs, menacing,
Strangle the trunk's innocent child.
Clawing the wood's neck,
He digs his nails beneath its skin
And it bleeds clumps
From its complexion.

He detects me spy upon
Evil carelessness
And glides from his stolen home.
He rests on the fence, glaring
Through beady bold eyes,
They unfold his ethereal facade.
His heavy black bills,
Short wiry feathers across his nostrils,
He retains his stare and it worries me,
Menacing to pounce.

His broad wings and rounded tail
Are weapons and now I have none.
A cunning, clever fellow,
I can only presume he plans his attack.
I foolishly wait and I am his audience
As he whistles unmelodious
And shrieks his caw song,
I wrinkle my nose and he grins.
The pest looks like a sultan
In the light of the sun.

His plumose coat shines like silk,
I am insignificant in his wraith.
He travels far but is not weak,
He elongates, shows villainous confidence,
And I baptize him lord of fowl, the Crow

The Sound of War

The earth tremors around me,
But I am stagnant as stone,
Like I am exempt.

The world powders,
As I pause and pursue
The surreal.

The rat-at-tat-tat,
Like the rhyme we learned
In Primary school.

Whimpers and howls,
As I remain dry-eyed,
Alone, released.

Like an earthquake,
Fissures, fires, slumps
In the ground, I once stood.

I cannot hear the river
Which once sang clear,
The songbirds have fled,

Rubble has surfaced
Like passionate ocean waves
Making love to the coast.

And smoke, everywhere,
Six billion smokers could
Not choke so much.

The fume is clouds
Gathering in looming gangs,
Clouds that will not rain-

Just linger like unreturned
Love. A goad of grey
Surrounding the sky.

No bodies, no souls.
It grows cold here
On the roof, alone.

I cannot feel fire below,
There are no voices,
There is no body heat.

All the cars are trodden now.
It has ended, with no one left.
No baking fire nor rat-at-tat-tat-

Only a stifle of grief
Like a woman with cats
Blistering for her sins.

And alone I last,
Through the sound of War,
Where there is no sorrow.

Theatre-Going

He dressed over-obviously
And pulled the door tight. And again,
Because this is the city.
One leg in, crouch, grunt, sigh, and sit
Into the comfortable Renault.
Two minutes and twenty four curses away
De la theatre, he arrives.
No such thing as too close to drive,
Too tight to park, bang! He wont notice that.
Late. It's five past eight. Throw a bucket
At the clerk, 'Might as well get rid of some my change.'
A glance to make sure no one saw that.
Sniff, tap tap tapidy tap of the finger
On the desk, waiting for bloody ages for
That stupid girl to count the eighteen euro
In twenties, even though he's already late.
'Cheers...' reconsidering... 'sweetheart'
By chance she favoured the older type...
In particular the pot belly, buckets of change,
The punctuality, sexy baldness
Not to mention sweat patches... reconsidering...
'That's a restricted seat on the balcony wing,
The left half of the stage can't be seen.
Our apologies. It's all we've got. Enjoy the show.'
He puts his blazer back on.
Pinstriped, for effect.
Creaks the well-oiled door... he thinks-
Fast and loud or slow and not so loud,

Must have chosen the latter as
It creaks for I-mean-ages! and then to the
'Sorry', 'sorry there', 'sorry', 'sorry, eh, sorry'
When one clear 'excuse me' would have worked.
It's started. Comedy. He laughs loud
And spits a lot. Wedged in between
A young guy and girl, who begin to flirt.
Some giggles, dirty looks, and nudges later
The over-dramatised, badly-characterised
Display of amateurism ends, and he follows
The crowd and stands up for all he's worth.
Shuffle. Keys. Ignition. Curse. Park. Home.
'Well. Tell me all about the show.'
The critic arrives, adds some self-adoring
Details, deletes some, laughs, milks, milks,
milks,
And then to bed, to think about the stage,
And the lights, to where the city is alive,
The standing ovation, the sheer drive,
And sure, he will go again.